Also by the Author

Awareness

Talks With Temerlen

The Heart of Awareness

Inside the Mind of Awareness

Transforming Negative Emotions

visit
PantheonProseBooks.com

the Quiet Place Within

Peter Ingle

Published in the United States of America
Library of Congress Cataloging-in-Publication Data

Ingle, Peter M.
The Quiet Place Within

There is a place in you where you
are quiet, calm, and nothing can disturb
you. This quiet place is not a metaphor.
It is a very real thing.

P.D. Ouspensky

Contents

Contents

Contents

Contents

Contents

7   **109**

Contents

The
Quiet Place
Within

1

There is within us something that
transcends all activity which is
unchanging, immovable, and
eternally at rest.

Swami Abhedananda

The Silent Void

THE quiet place within is a void of pure awareness that cannot be seen or heard by the mind, and cannot be felt by the body. When this void is aware *of* things, it is called consciousness. When it is aware *of itself,* it is called presence. And when it is *aware of being aware,* it is called conscious awareness.

Everything awareness is aware of appears inside its field of consciousness. This includes thoughts, emotions, sensations, inner voices, visions, inspiration, insight, movement, nature, people—*everything* in both the inner and the outer world.

Awareness itself is not inside the field of its perception. It *is* the perception comprising the field. This quiet 'place' is formless, motionless, silent, undisturbed, impenetrable, and unknown—until it knows *itself* as pure awareness.

Invisible to Itself

AWARENESS is invisible to everything it perceives, and even invisible to itself. Precisely because it *is* perception, it cannot be perceived. But it can realize itself *as* perception.

Awareness is also not what the mind experiences as attention, even though awareness can extend itself through attention. But when this happens without awareness being there *at the same time*, attention is an activity of only the mind.

Interestingly, the substance of attention is visible in the sense that you can feel when you focus attention. It becomes mentally tangible, almost palpable. Yet there is something else behind attention and that something else is either aware of being there or not. It is always there, but it is not usually aware of being there. And even when it is aware of being aware, it is still invisible to itself.

Tranquility

AWARENESS is always perfectly tranquil. It is not a quiet mind or a calm body, and even when those are not quiet or calm, awareness remains tranquil.

This tranquility is like a bubble that nothing seen or felt can penetrate. It is there at the core of your being, and it is there surrounding you. In both cases, it is simply a perspective of perception. Its only activity and only purpose is to be the seer. *Everything* else appears and disappears in its sight while it remains empty, silent, motionless, and unreactive in the background.

This bubble of tranquility is where awareness realizes itself as awareness.

Attachment

ALTHOUGH awareness is its own sanctuary, it can be lured out of its 'place' by anything it perceives. Due to a lack of awareness that it *is* awareness, it gets immediately appropriated by whatever it perceives.

In human beings, awareness is first appropriated by thoughts, emotions, sensations, and movements. Instead of awareness seeing all of these functions and knowing that it is seeing them, it grants them identity as a sense of 'me'.

In the East, this is known as 'attachment' to describe how awareness attaches itself to its perceptions. In the West, it is called 'identification' to convey that awareness not only attaches itself *to*, but establishes a sense of identity *in*, what it perceives.

All of this usually happens so quickly that we don't notice it, and we don't notice it because awareness is not noticing itself.

Finding Itself

BECAUSE awareness does not 'remember' itself as awareness, it knows itself only *in relation to* what it perceives.

Periodically, however, awareness discovers itself in the quiet of its own domain. When this happens, we experience an absence of thought, expectation, resistance, fear, and time.

But because we are not accustomed to this emptiness, it can be as disorienting as it is wonderful. Before we fully realize what has happened, awareness lapses out of itself and back into identification, and we imperceptibly move on with our lives.

Out of Silence

EVERYTHING comes out of inner silence so rapidly that its origin is barely noticeable. A tiny impulse flashes with a lightning-fast burst that we experience as a sensation. As quickly as it appears, the sensation speeds through our inner world and ignites a thought or feeling which informs our outlook, shapes our decision-making, and steers our behavior.

This chain of events happens differently when awareness is not attached to it. Awareness 'remembers' itself and remains consciously aware as impulses arise, as the mind reacts, and as the body engages.

After impulses, thoughts, and movements have finished their journey through the mind and body, conscious awareness watches them disappear into the same empty silence they came from.

Into Sound

WIND instruments beautifully convey how sound emerges from silence because their 'music' is produced by the breathing out of the musician. By means of breath, cascades of sound tumble out of silence and into sound in a way that reflects the emptiness—the vastness—of its origin.

The same is true of the highest expressions of artistic creation, whose form manages to emanate the formlessness of the awareness that gave birth to the form. It is this quality, more than the form it takes, which makes art great. Why? Because it comes as close as form can to transmitting the mystery of its source—which is the deepest purpose of the arts in this world.

Most musicians, actors, painters, and poets fill the form of their art with themselves and their identity (their 'personal' expression), rather than allowing the vast formlessness of awareness to shine through them. When it does, however, they experience the true transformation of art.

Stillness and Silence

STILLNESS and silence are two attributes of awareness. When we reach stillness, we approach silence. When we reach silence, we approach stillness.

When stillness and silence comingle, they create a perfect environment for awareness to become aware of being aware. But they are only the environment. Awareness still has to emerge there.

Untellable

THE light of the sun renders everything on earth visible and alive. Yet this light is not the sun; it comes *from* the sun; it is a byproduct of the sun. The sun itself is something more.

In a similar way, awareness renders everything visible and 'alive' to our perception, yet awareness itself is something more than perception. This something includes a capacity to be aware of being aware as the perceiver *and* as the source of perception.

This inner light of perception is invisible, inaudible, and intangible to the mind and senses. Walt Whitman called it, "Light rare untellable, lighting the very light."

Surpassing Understanding

THERE are many references in The New Testament about the nature of awareness. One of the most beautiful is, "The peace of God, which passeth all understanding."

Peace suggests calm and quiet. God suggests great love, care, and protection. Together, they intimate the essence of awareness.

The second phrase, however—"which passeth all understanding"—refers to a very distinct aspect of awareness, which is that it lies beyond the mind's ability to comprehend it. This is because awareness is not a compartment in the mind; it does not happen in the mind or to the mind. It resides in a different dimension. It *is* that other dimension.

The mind can think about the *idea* of that dimension, but it can never understand it.

2

When you look from emptiness
you see everything.

H.W. L. Poonja

Meditation, Yoga, and Prayer

QUIET, calm, and peace are often associated with meditation, yoga, and prayer—yet in all three an important ingredient is often missing. This 'ingredient' involves a subtle shift from the meditator *in* the mind to the meditator *as* silent awareness; from maintaining a posture to witnessing the posture and realizing yourself as the witness; from reciting prayer to using prayer as leverage for awareness.

Although meditation, yoga, and prayer can quiet the mind, pacify the body, and evoke a feeling of peace, their greatest value does not lie in mastering a mantra or posture or prayer. It lies in how well they enable the mind and body to yield themselves *on behalf of* awareness. Yoga is the body quieting itself and indirectly quieting the thinking mind. Meditation is the thinking mind quieting itself and indirectly quieting the body. Prayer is the emotional mind quieting itself and indirectly quieting the thinking mind and the body. All three may be inspired by awareness, but none of them come from, and none of them are performed by, awareness.

Satipatthana

THIS is the Buddhist word for meditation. Its etymology translates as *sati* ('remember' or 'recollect') and *upatthana* ('awareness' or 'presence').

Remember awareness.
Remember presence.
Recollect awareness.
Recollect presence.

The true nature of meditation is not about the mind speaking to itself or trying to encourage your person to remember yourself. It is about the mind appealing *to* awareness and trying to evoke the awareness of awareness:

"Remember your awareness, awareness."
"Recollect your presence, awareness."
"Remember yourself as awareness."

The Muscle of Attention

WHEN the mind controls attention, it thinks it is controlling awareness. It does not realizing that it *cannot* comprehend what awareness really is.

Focusing attention is something the muscle of the mind does. It involves a narrowing of attention the way you narrow the stream of light from a flashlight by turning the barrel of the flashlight. The mind knows it can 'turn' itself to focus the stream of attention, but it does not understand the light—the awareness—passing *through* it.

Awareness itself is so rarefied that it cannot be contained by the mind or the body. It can pass through them and vivify them, but they cannot hold it or control it. The only thing that can contain awareness is itself, and it does not 'do' that through mental or physical effort. It simply becomes aware that it is aware.

Amen

THE last word in The Lord's Prayer and many other prayers is 'Amen' which means "let it be so."

Letting things be usually implies the mind letting things out 'there' be as they are without any inducement to change them. This is indeed one of the meanings of 'Amen', but there is another meaning which has to do, not with things out there, but with awareness itself.

It means *being* the 'there' where everything happens, and at the same time welcoming everything as it comes out of awareness, appears in awareness, and resolves into awareness.

In The Lord's Prayer, Amen encapsulates the entire prayer, which is an appeal by the mind to awareness: "May awareness be itself and simply see things, internally and externally, without becoming identified with any of them."

For awareness, this means remaining aware in the purest, most conscious sense. For the mind, it means adopting a mental posture of acceptance that will promote awareness.

The Kingdom

HOW large is the inner world? Does it have boundaries? Do we know our location in it at all times? Why do we dwell in some regions, thoughts, and moods, and not in others? Most importantly, how is that we are able to perceive this inner world?

These are not common questions, mainly because the mind does not know itself. Something else has to know it. Something else has to see it and be aware of seeing it.

It is like asking the planets who they are, where they are, and what they are about. Meanwhile, the sun realizes that it alone can see the whole solar system and know itself as the source.

Self-realization is profound on the scale of a human being. Imagine it on the scale of a solar system, a galaxy, a cluster of galaxies, or the universe as a whole? It is the same awareness, only more expansive and more able to merge with the absolute awareness of the universe.

Space and Time

THE notion of a quiet place within supposes space, which in turn supposes time.

Space and time appear vivid in the physical world of objects, but get foggy in the psychological world of thoughts, feelings, moods, and hopes. Common to both worlds, however, is a sense of movement. Something is always moving in and *through* both worlds.

This is not true in the world of awareness where space vanishes and time disappears. Everything within awareness keeps moving and changing, but awareness does neither. It does not go anywhere in space or do anything in time. It simply *is* the higher dimension in which space and time play themselves out.

Inside-Out

THE more awareness realizes itself beyond the mind and the body, the farther it 'pops' out of both. Instead of experiencing itself inside the mind and next to thoughts, awareness discovers that it encompasses them.

The same thing happens to the meditator and the yogi. Instead of being them, awareness sees them meditating and doing yoga *inside of* itself.

It eventually becomes clear that we as people are not passing through our lives. Our lives and person are passing through awareness.

You Are the Sky

THE Buddha is purported to have said, "You are the sky. Everything else is the weather." What a beautiful image of the purity and vastness of awareness. How well it renders secondary the 'weather' of our inner world.

Compared to the earth, the sky is empty, formless, invisible, and 'beyond' the earth. The higher you go, the more empty, formless, and invisible the sky becomes as it merges with the next world above it, surrounding it. And so it goes with each higher realm in the universe, up to and including the mystery of infinity.

Miraculously, the 'sky' begins for us in the smaller but no less mysterious experience of simple, silent awareness. It is so simple and so silent that it goes unnoticed by the 'weather' in our mind and body, both of which have little knowledge of awareness, negligible interest in it, and no concern about it as they pursue themselves and their needs.

Being in the Moment

SOME people are naturally more active and some naturally more passive. For example, active types tend to *pursue* the moment and move *through* it with determination and goals, whereas passive types tend to *resist* the moment and be *pulled* by it despite their inertia. It is virtually impossible for either type to do otherwise, and it is easy to see why each has a different concept of what it means to be *in the moment.*

The moment, however, is neither active nor passive. It never insists on being pursued, manipulated, resisted, or avoided. That is just how each person interprets the moment and imposes requirements on the moment—either by looking for and clutching something to do, or by avoiding things and having to do them.

This does not mean that you should not be active or passive. It means that whatever your tendency is, awareness simply perceives that, watches it unfold as part of the moment, and realizes itself watching.

Being in Awareness

Awareness is not in the moment. The moment is in awareness. Everything it perceives is simply there as part of itself. From this perspective, it is not a matter of being in the moment. It is a matter of being awareness and embracing everything that comes into it.

The Empty Place

WHEN trying to envision the 'quiet place within' it is tempting to think of a spot with psychological coordinates. Where exactly is it? Finding this place is made more difficult by the fact that it is empty and not really a place. It is awareness itself, yet the mind can only conceptualize the idea of awareness, so it thinks in terms of an object in a 'place'.

It may help the mind to think of the quiet place as a bubble at the core of your being from which awareness peers out, and to know that no thought, emotion, or sensation can penetrate or disturb that bubble.

It is also possible to turn the bubble inside-out and conceive of it as all the empty space in your mind and body, and to regard it just like all the empty space in the universe.

Awareness can also be thought of as a boundless bubble, inside of which mind, body, and the universe all exist.

Abundance

TRUE abundance is not material or physical. It is a void that is able to contain everything because it is always empty.

This void does not seek to hold onto anything or to fill itself. As a result, everything can pass through it and experience a feeling of abundance as it does. Yet what passes through and what is aware of it passing through are not the same: one is *always* empty.

This is why it feels so good to let go of physical and psychological attachments. Letting go immediately brings us closer to the void and to consciousness of the void, which always has a familiar feeling of the unknown about it.

In a Mood

IT is common to say that we are 'in' a mood, as though a mood is a place inside where we go and get bogged down.

Although different moods exist, look carefully and you will see that you are not in them, but that they are in you; that moods unfold inside awareness and awareness attaches itself *to* them.

This is not to say that moods should be eradicated or that it is easy for awareness to extricate itself from them. It is just important to know the difference between a mood and being aware of a mood, and to know that awareness can free *itself* from any mood at any moment.

One way to see this is to not let anyone see when you are in a bad mood; to not display and express the bad mood. Instead, try to keep it inside and look at it there. Then realize the difference between the mood and looking at it.

3

Ultimately you come to something
so simple that there are no words
to express it.

Nisargadatta

Transformation

ONE of the key ideas of the fourth way tradition is that awakening (self-realization) revolves around the transformation of negative emotions. This refers to all emotions that carry a negative charge such as irritation, impatience, boredom, self-pity, resentment, hatred, and anger—to name just a few.

Indulging in negative emotions inwardly and venting them outwardly are usually considered normal, even healthy manifestations of human character. The fourth way, however, takes the position that they are abnormal because they corrupt and consume awareness. The idea behind withholding the outer expression of negative emotions is to wedge open a psychological window through which you can look at a negative emotion and examine 'who' is negative *on the inside.*

As with moods, the goal is not to ignore or suppress negative emotions inwardly. The purpose is to withhold their outer expression and use that as leverage to shine light on the logic behind them. When awareness realizes itself as the observer shining this light, it begins to transmute the sense of 'I' behind negativity into the awareness of *itself* as the conscious observer. In this sense, transformation is not about negative emotions being transformed into something else; it is about awareness using negative emotions and the feeling of 'I' behind them as a catalyst to transform itself.

In this sense, transformation can occur in relation to *anything* as soon as awareness realizes that it is outside that thing. This is because being aware of being aware *is* transformation and is what makes transformation possible.

Symptoms of Identification

IDENTIFICATION is more than what it appears because although awareness is what *becomes* identified, it is the mind and body which react to it and show the symptoms of awareness having lost awareness of itself.

When identification happens, the substance of awareness pours into the mind and body, but they are the wrong kinds of engines for that kind of fuel. It is almost like the mind eating gas and the body drinking electricity. The result is 'disturbance' in their normal operations which we experience as feeling flustered, hurried, forceful, zealous, insistent, and volatile. Identification infiltrates all our thoughts, feelings, sensations, and actions and makes us feel as though we *the person* are identified.

It then seems logical that if we can control these symptoms we will become enlightened. In the end, however, it is awareness that has to realize *and* cure the illness *at its source.*

The Person

THE person we are as a mind and body has nothing—*nothing*—to do with awareness. More accurately, awareness has nothing to do with our person. But because of how the mind and body reflect and interpret awareness, it becomes something they then try to achieve as a person.

When the mind encounters the concept of awareness, it thinks it *knows* how to be aware. Similarly, the body is sure that it can *feel* awareness. But as remarkable as the mind and body are, they can at best be conduits *through which* awareness realizes itself.

As Jean Klein said: "Liberation is not of the person. It is freedom from the person."

Leaving the Person Behind

WE all live in the same outer world, yet we each live in a different inner world. The combination of our thoughts, feelings, and predispositions varies from one person to another and becomes the material out of which we develop a sense of ourselves as a person.

At the same time, each person is loathe to acknowledge that their *entire* inner world does not matter and can be left behind; not abandoned, but revealed as a false sense of self that is not awareness.

The more awareness is conscious of itself, the less interest it takes in the machinations of the mind and the preoccupations of the body, and the more interest it takes in the mystery of awareness beyond the mind and body.

Stages of Self Remembering

THE central idea of the fourth way is called self-remembering, which refers to awareness being consciously aware of being aware. But self-remembering does not always start on the level of awareness. It often starts on a physical level, then expands to a psychological level, before reaching the metaphysical presence of awareness being aware.

The reason self-remembering starts physically is because it is taught as a principle of *external* divided attention where, for example, you are aware not only of the sunset but of yourself watching the sunset. Instead of there being one thing in your attention, there are now two. This dividing of attention *by* the mind starts to mirror the nature of awareness.

Divided attention can also be brought *inside* the mind. Instead of being absorbed by thoughts and feelings (and negative emotions), you 'divide attention' and watch your thoughts. This form of dividing attention *internally* is closer to the realm of awareness. It contains the seed of awareness, but it is still the mind controlling attention in the mind.

The House

ENVISION your mind as a house with many rooms. Inside one room is a collection of thoughts, concepts, and ideas; inside another a collection of worries, fears, and hopes; inside another sensations and dreads; and inside yet another a portfolio of plans and projects waiting to be done.

Each of the occupants in these rooms exist as an image of 'I', and they can each roam throughout the house either randomly, harmoniously, or in conflict with one another.

Meanwhile, awareness is the empty space inside *and* outside the house. This all-encompassing emptiness can become aware of being aware of everything in the house.

Awareness Asleep

ALMOST every moment, awareness attaches itself to and identifies itself with one 'I' or a group of 'I's. They become 'me' for as long as awareness stays attached and until it is lured by another 'I'. And so we go from attachment to attachment, day after day, in our inner and outer world.

The fourth way calls this being 'asleep', meaning that awareness has forgotten itself and lost the realization that it is awareness. It is hypnotized by and literally asleep *in* the mind and body.

We are usually not consciously aware of our body in the environment, or consciously aware of thoughts and feelings in the mind. Least of all are we consciously aware of being the observer of both worlds.

When awareness remembers itself, it wakes up from the dream of mind and body and realizes itself as awareness.

What Am I

WE rarely question that our body developed from a tiny cell inside another body before emerging in the physical world where it grows, matures, weakens, and withers before finally disappearing into the void from which it came.

Even less do we examine the nature of our psychological life: that in addition to the external world, we live amidst ever-shifting thoughts, feelings, opinions, imaginings, hopes, and fears—all the while capable of language, equations, reason, wonder, and the arts.

Least of all do we question awareness: that we can be aware of our body moving, aware of our mind turning, and aware of existing on the thin edge of a planet in the universe.

What is this body, what is the mind, what is the universe, and what is awareness? Why do we not rigorously investigate these? Only when awareness becomes aware of being aware do these mysteries flood into perception and astonish.

Who You Are

IF you could draw a picture of your mind, what would it look like? Where would everything be located? Is the architecture the same for everyone? Where are its boundaries?

What about the feeling of 'you' inside the mind? What is that exactly? Where does it come from? How does it form? Does it reside in a specific place? Why does it feel proud, hurt, happy, threatened, sad, isolated, at peace? What is happening when 'you' morph into so many shapes, moods, and meanings?

The truth is that the mind cannot answer these questions because it does not have the *capacity* to be aware of itself. Something else has that capacity.

That something else is a higher dimension encompassing the mind and body. Although this dimension cannot see itself, it can *realize* itself by being aware that it is aware. This is the only thing in creation that can do this, which is why existence as a human being is so precious and profound.

The Self

THE word 'self' is confusing because it is sometimes spelled with a small 's' to signify the ego, and sometimes with a capital 'S' to signify the enlightened 'Self'. The mind construes from this that large Self is simply an improved version of small self, a more 'mindful' version, a more enlightened *person*.

The small self exists as a feeling of 'I' in the mind and as a sense of 'me' in the body, but there is no such feeling in awareness. It just *is*. It exists as a void of presence that is aware of seeing the mind and body as they function.

Unlike the mind, awareness does not conceptualize or project an identity of itself; and unlike the body, it does not occupy space. It is more akin to a non-self that is aware of being aware of the self.

The Curious Mind

WHEN awareness slips free of the mind and achieves the clarity of being aware of being aware, this inevitably prompts the mind to wonder about awareness, to want to investigate it, define it, and be able to explain its meaning, purpose, and origin.

All of this is a distraction to awareness because it draws awareness right back into the mind. Awareness has to keep dropping the mind and keep abiding in the mystery of itself.

Into the Distance

LOOK out at the sea or into the sky as far as you can. Then consider that your inner world is infinitely more vast than that.

Most of the time we stay close to shore, hug the surface, cling to the familiar and safe. This is not a bad thing; it just prevents us from realizing how much we contain inside and how far we can go—even with the vehicle of thought, which is more nimble than we suspect.

At a certain point, however, thought reaches its limit. It simply cannot go farther or comprehend more. It cannot venture into the increasing emptiness and darkness where there are no forms, concepts, or words. Only awareness can roam that distance and navigate those depths.

Supporting Awareness

WHEN awareness is consciously aware, we notice many more things and we see them in a new way, with a clearer, deeper perception.

Knowing this and also knowing when awareness is less conscious, we can use the mind and body to prompt awareness by intentionally heightening attention in the five senses. For example, by putting more attention into looking around, tasting our food, smelling the soap, feeling the handrail, and hearing the sounds nearby.

Purposely focusing attention is a way of harnessing the mind and body in support of awareness, as a conduit for awareness to flow through, as a container in which it can *re*-collect itself and *re*-member itself as awareness.

Our Branch in This Universe

WHAT we call the universe is more complex than our science can discern. For example, the known universe may be just one branch among many on a single tree; and there may be multiple trees in the forest of an extended universe or even series of universes.

Universes may also vary; some with no branches, like a palm tree; and some with multiple branches, like an oak. Meanwhile, our planet is a small one in one solar system within just one galaxy.

The Inquiry

THE quiet place within of awareness never asks, "who am I?"

Behind the body is the mind. Behind the mind is a mental projection of 'me'. Behind all of these is awareness.

Everything ultimately points to awareness.

4

We are always the Self,
only we do not realize it.

Ramana Maharshi

48

Through the Eyes

LIGHT reflects off objects and conveys those reflections to the eyes which send them through the orbital nerve to the brain. The brain itself does not see the objects but is instead shown a reflected image of them on its inner screen.

Eyesight is a marvel in all living creatures, yet human vision is unique because whereas the eyes of animals serve to safeguard their existence, human eyes do more; they not only receive impressions of light, those impressions evoke thoughts and mental associations. Human eyes can also transmit emotions to other humans. If we could follow in slow-motion everything that unfolds in a human glance, we would be astonished at the connection between eye, brain, emotions, and back again.

Most astonishing, however, is the role that our eyes play in self-realization. They enable awareness to realize itself as that which is looking at creation *through* our eyes.

The Mouth of Awareness

AWARENESS might be said to feed off of light because so many perceptions that reach awareness and arouse awareness are transmitted by light.

In the case of light coming *into* awareness, our physical eyes are like a mouth where the impression of light enters before reaching the brain. But for impressions of light to reach their deepest possible destination, we have to do more than open our eyes. We have to *knowingly look* at our physical and psychological worlds. Then we have to chew and taste: we have to become *aware of looking*. Then we have to swallow: we have to become *aware of being aware* as we look.

When awareness is not aware of itself *while* looking, we see things without truly noticing them, and life gets merely lived.

Held in Check

WHEN the mind and body look at people, they perceive physical features, magnetism, mannerisms, and idiosyncrasies. When awareness looks at people, it perceives awareness held in check by a sense of 'I' in the person. And sometimes it perceives itself.

Pure Seeing

IN most moments, as soon as reflections of light pass into our eyes, they get filtered in the brain as thoughts, emotions, and sensations. This happens so fast that we do not *fully* see the impressions being delivered by light; we see instead what gets imposed on them by our filters.

A simple example is when we look at a tree: instead of seeing a mystery of nature with a unique essence that manufacturers chlorophyll and is a home for animals, a source of fuel and lumber, and a canopy for shade, we *mentally* label it as 'tree' and move on. We look at it without seeing it. Sometimes our filters are so preoccupied that we do not even see what is right *in front of us.*

Try to notice what is around you. As you do, notice the barrage of thoughts interfering with *seeing*—to the point that you forget altogether that you were trying to notice what is around you. There are so many things we don't *truly* notice: things like grass, flowers, stones, water, animals, people, clouds, sunlight, the moon. Most of all, we don't notice that we are *able* to notice them.

Sea Mind

THOUGHT, emotion, sensation, intuition, insight, and attraction—all of these represent different 'I's swimming in the sea of our mind where the water is sometimes calm, sometimes turbulent, and always changing.

Some 'I's swim near the surface of the mind, some lurk at the bottom. Some appear in groups, some alone. Meanwhile, all of them and the water they swim in are held by a sea bed that never moves, never interferes, and is never noticed by the fish or the water. This is awareness beyond the mind.

The universe is similar, where planets and galaxies are like fish and schools of fish, and space is like water. Beyond them, encompassing them, yet unnoticed by them, is an eternal quietude that is aware of being aware of everything inside it.

The Source

MANKIND does not fully understand light or electricity. We know that these phenomena exist, but not exactly how and why.

What if something in the universe is faster, brighter, and stronger than light; so fast, bright, and full of energy that we cannot perceive or measure it? For instance, we still don't know *for certain* what lies deep beneath the sun's surface or at its core, or how the sun came to be, or exactly how it operates. Nor do we know the nature of our galaxy's core and the mysteries containing it.

In the same way, and for the same reasons, the mind cannot perceive the hidden mystery of awareness.

Reflections of Awareness

THE light of the sun renders everything on earth visible and gives it 'life'. Awareness does the same thing in relation to what we perceive in our internal and external world.

Everything seen by awareness also gets reflected back—via the light seeing it—to its source. In other words, everything awareness sees is actually a reflection of *itself*. Whatever it sees, it is always seeing itself. And whenever it is aware of being aware, it is realizing itself.

This sounds ludicrous to the mind. It sounds like a mental trick of some sort, but it is not. Awareness is in everything, and everything is an extension of awareness. But only in the source of itself is it aware of this.

Brighter and Brighter

LIKE light, awareness has the inevitable tendency to shine farther and embrace more. Its very nature in our case is to expand beyond the confines of a person always thinking about himself and dwelling on herself.

Awareness does not *want* to see more and expand more. It *is* seeing and expansion. And the thing it is most looking for and expanding into is itself.

Transcending Negativity

THE fourth way distinguishes between negative and positive emotions, and proposes that the former can be transformed into the latter by mastering the science of not expressing negative emotions *outwardly* and the art of transcending them *inwardly*.

The principle of transformation comprises a lengthy topic, but it can be condensed into two key points. One is that all negative emotions are a form of rejection and negation *by* the mind, whereas positive emotions are a form of pure perception *through* the mind. It is not just that emotions are negative (unpleasant) or positive (pleasant); it is that they carry opposite electrical charges: one which pushes perception away and one that pulls it toward.

The other key point is that negative emotions develop in the mind and get expressed by the body, whereas transformation occurs in awareness. Negative emotions that are contained and not expressed become a catalyst for awareness to contain *itself* and realize itself as pure awareness.

Out of the Cocoon

DUE to attachment, awareness gets lured out of its 'place'. It gets siphoned away *unaware* to become identified with phenomena. Such is the nature of human existence on earth.

This same existence, however, includes the potential for awareness to escape the pull of attachment and realize the truth about itself as awareness. Each of us is a psychological and physical cocoon in which the caterpillar can become a butterfly.

Wordless

THE transformation of negative emotions, as well as the transformation of deep suffering, begins *and* ends wordlessly.

It begins with the wordless non-expression of negative emotions so that their 'substance' can be used internally as a catalyst.

It ends as the wordless transmutation of awareness conscious as itself.

Non Violence

ALL negative emotions are violent to some degree. The ultimate degree is when one human kills another human, thus destroying the possibility of awareness realizing itself through that person.

By contrast, the ultimate form of non-violence is being aware of being aware. Just pure perception seeing creation without interfering with it.

Some may call this passive compliance with the evils of the world, but that demonstrates a lack of understanding about the world, its apparent evils, and how both are tied to the larger wheel of the universe.

As Epictetus said, "Seek not to have things happen as you choose. Rather choose to have them happen as they do. And so shall you live prosperously."

The Height

THE height of existence is not to be *in* the moment. The height is to *be* the awareness in which the moment is always unfolding.

The mind and body exist in the moment. They manifest in the moment, but they are not the awareness in which they keep unfolding. Neither the present moment nor the things that happen in the moment are the awareness that encompasses them.

The Incubator

THE mind and body serve as an incubator for awareness. They are a medium in which awareness can contain itself, reflect perception back to itself, and realize itself. This is what makes the experience of being a human being so remarkable and, as far as we can tell, unique in the universe.

It is also noteworthy that the body is visible and tangible, which is the nature of the physical realm. Meanwhile, the mind is visible but intangible. We can see thoughts with our inner vision, but we cannot touch them. Such is the nature of the psychological realm.

Beyond both the physical and psychological realms lies the metaphysical realm of awareness which is so rarefied that it is both invisible and intangible. Such is the nature of an *entirely different* dimension.

The body is like the land and ocean. Thoughts are like birds in flight. Awareness is like the empty sky whose boundary knows no limit. And just as the earth's atmosphere serves as an incubator for life, so we as *humans* serve as an incubator for the *being* of awareness.

Walking into Awareness

THE next time you go for a walk, leave your person, problems, and plans at home. Simply look *through* your eyes and be aware of looking. Just notice what is around you as you walk.

Treat your walk as a journey into awareness. Walk slowly. Make where you are your sole destination as you walk. Instead of going somewhere, be where you are going at each step. Allow awareness to settle into itself and to set your pace.

When you look from awareness with awareness, you don't have to reach out and grab things with your vision. Everything will bring itself and present itself to awareness (which never goes anywhere).

You can even think of your entire life as a slow walk where what you do and what you see is important only in relation to the degree to which awareness is consciously aware of it. Like walking, our life is not about achieving and arriving. It is about awareness realizing itself, which is the highest purpose and meaning of life.

Presence First

A TURNAROUND happens when instead of trying to be present while living your life, you start living your life while being present. Instead of fitting awareness into your activities, you fit everything into awareness. You wake up in the morning with awareness *first* and everything else in your day unfolds and transpires within the envelope of awareness.

Whatever happens, awareness becomes your touchstone, your reference point, and your retreat. As the temptations of mind, body, and life around you still try to lure you out of awareness, you know better; you stay home in the quiet place within and just watch.

Layers of Identity

MIND, body, and awareness are layers of identity superimposed on each other. When awareness is not conscious of itself, these layers flatten into what feels like one layer—one sense of self.

As awareness becomes aware of being aware, the layers start to separate, but the moment awareness forgets itself, the layers collapse into each other again.

The thickest and most visible layer is our body with its actions and reactions. Behind it is a thinner, less visible layer of thoughts and emotions and inner sensations. We usually feel these two layers of mind and body as one sense of 'me'.

Behind both is an even thinner and more transparent membrane, which is the 'image' of who we believe ourselves to be. This image is a hologram that the mind projects internally, and like a hologram it can never be grasped because *it is not real.* It is a psychological fabrication, and even though we think it is the 'person' that we project to the world, it is not. Who we imagine ourselves to be as this membrane on the inside and how the world sees us on the outside are very different, which is one reason why it is alarming to see ourselves in a picture or video (and sometimes in the mirror, which is a reverse image).

The hologram of 'I' *is* the ego, and it persists as a mental image even as we try to be aware and to observe the mind and body. It persists because it is so thin and so transparent (and therefore hard to perceive), and because it lies just next to awareness.

In this sense, awareness is like the light in a projector whereas the ego-hologram is like the film in front of the light, through which the light passes. Imprinted on the film are thoughts, emotions, and sensations which ultimately get projected as actions and reactions onto the screen of our life.

Awareness is not the film, or the contents of the film, or the projection of those contents. It is the pure light *and* the empty screen. But when it is unaware of itself, it cannot distinguish itself from everything else. Even when awareness manages to distinguish itself, it has a hard time realizing itself apart from the film. This is why it is easy to keep an 'enlightened' ego, which is still part of the hologram.

5

Few cross over the river.
Most are stranded on this side.
Seek rather the other shore.

Buddha

Finding and Realizing

AWARENESS initially finds itself in the physical world. It realizes it is in a body and is *aware of* the body. Then awareness finds itself in the psychological world. It realizes it is in the mind *seeing* the mind. Then awareness finds itself outside both body and mind. It realizes it is inside the natural world on earth, and that it is neither of those either.

At each stage, awareness 'pops' out of the previous world as it realizes itself perceiving it. What then of the solar system, the galaxy, and beyond? What will awareness be as it pops out of each of those worlds?

Look at your life thus far and at all the changes you have encountered in the body, in the mind, in the world. What one thing has not changed throughout all those changes? What one thing is always there in the background, *as* the background, already outside of everything?

Mysterious Resolution

OUR body, mind, and whole life appear out of nothing and slowly disappear into nowhere. The same is true about solar systems and galaxies.

The whole creation is a breathtaking mystery; our existence in it even more so. Behind both is the even greater mystery of awareness being aware of creation and existence. This sacred phenomenon of awareness can perceive that everything which has appeared in creation is gradually resolving into the awareness that sees it. The more this happens, the more awareness realizes itself as the mystery behind everything.

The Edge of Negativity

WHEN we feel negative—from minor impatience to extreme anger—it seems as though we have reached a limit; that we have gone as far as we can go and have no choice but to indulge in the reaction and vent our feelings.

Go deeper, however, and you will discover that this is not true. There is more internal territory to explore *beyond* whatever negative emotion is circulating. This is true of volatile negative emotions as well as the embers of bitterness, self-pity, and resentment.

Indulging in negative emotions inwardly and expressing them outwardly are *automatic* reactions. The first is psychological and happens instantaneously. The second is physical and gains velocity through expression. Restraining and going beyond both means jumping into awareness *as* awareness.

Try to remember that there is a door which lies just beyond the point where you feel the impulse to indulge in negative emotions and the urge to express them. That door is the beginning of a vast inner terrain where only awareness can roam.

The Butterfly

THE purpose of not expressing negative emotions outwardly is to contain the ego, the sense of 'me'—not for the purpose of squashing or suppressing feelings, but to cast light on the 'me' behind them. This opportunity is lost as soon as a negative emotion is expressed because at that point it enters the physical world and leaves a footprint of 'me'.

Containing negative emotions and shining the light of awareness on them inside reveals the workings of the ego. It exposes the deeper sense of 'me' behind the rationale of negativity. By containing the expression of 'me' and exposing its inner logic, awareness starts to 'cross over'—to transform—from 'me feeling negative' to an awareness of being aware of 'me' and its presumed negativity.

Just as the caterpillar disintegrates in the cocoon and emerges as a butterfly, the ego simultaneously dissolves *in* awareness and induces the self-realization *of* awareness.

The Prism

AWARENESS peers out at the world through the prism of mind and body. Normally unaware of itself, it manifests through the inner world of thoughts and feelings before *becoming* the actions of a person in the outer world.

What starts as pure perception gets appropriated by viewpoints, expectations, bodily needs, preferences, and the myriad influences of whatever cultural web we are swept into. Within the flash of each moment, awareness morphs out of itself and into the identity of a person without ever stopping to examine the process.

As awareness becomes more aware of being aware, the realization grows that 'I' am not my life, that 'I' am not this person, that 'I' am not these thoughts and emotions; that 'I' am the awareness seeing them and aware of seeing them.

Instead of looking through a prism and knowing itself only *in relation to* things, awareness starts to know itself directly as awareness and to see everything else from awareness.

Awareness in Others

WHEN we drive on a busy road, we usually notice other cars but not the drivers. Nor do they see us. It's as if each car has a persona through which it relates to the other cars.

The same thing is true of people. Our personalities are what interact and maneuver. Rarely are we aware of something behind our own eyes, and rarely do we glimpse that something *in* another person.

Compared to the rigidity of cars, human beings are delicate, especially on the inside. This is particularly true about the 'substance' of awareness. Even though this substance cannot be seen with the physical eyes, it radiates an effervescence that can fill with 'presence' when awareness is aware of itself.

This does not mean we should go looking for awareness in everyone or try to manifest presence for others to notice. That won't work. But it does mean that we can 'remember' this awareness in ourselves and in others, and act accordingly.

Minding Maladies

There are no maladies in the stillness of awareness. Maladies exist in the mind and in the body, and it is alright for them to exist there because they have a function of their own. And although the mind and body may try—and even should try—to eliminate their maladies, that is never the responsibility of awareness.

It is also true that the more awareness knows itself, and the less attached it is to the mind and body, the more it 'enables' maladies to diminish, dissolve, and even disappear. This is particularly true of maladies that are mind-made; that are entirely imagined and reinforced to foster the ego.

The less awareness invests in our troubles, sickness, worries, and fears, the more these things lose their place of importance at the center of our being. If we can just see our maladies without giving them expression, this can serve as a springboard for awareness to realize itself as the neutral witness of our life.

Comingling

THE imperfection of awareness is the innocence with which it yields itself to thoughts, feelings, sensations, opinions, beliefs, people, events—everything. The tendency to slip out of itself and into other things happens only because awareness is not being aware of *itself*. When it *is* aware of being aware, it still extends itself to things but without instilling itself in them.

When awareness remains conscious of itself while perceiving, it can consciously comingle with everything else. It can enter into things and 'know' them without losing knowledge of itself.

The reality of this is beyond description and beyond the mind's attempts to experience it. It is the property of another realm *in which* awareness sees everything and *through which* everything reveals itself to awareness.

The Impalpable Mystery

AWARENESS is the greatest mystery of the known universe. The mere existence of the universe and the fact that we can be aware of it are already mind-boggling. But even more remarkable is that we can be aware of being aware of the universe; that we can be a conscious observer of creation.

This surely runs at the deepest current of the universe. It is where we penetrate the world of light and even go beyond light to where light and awareness *become* possible.

What is that? What is the inherent nature of this most significant yet least palpable reality that is behind everything else in the universe?

The Unfolding of the Mind

IT is tempting to believe that we 'think' thoughts and 'perceive' with emotions. It is hard to realize that thoughts and emotions follow perception and form *in response to* perception as interpretations and reactions.

This is noteworthy in relation to negative emotions because when awareness is not bound to the mind and body by identification, we do not have negative emotions. They have no place or material with which to form. As a result, everything we perceive simply folds up into conscious awareness.

Pressure

PRESSURE comes to us in the form of pain, anxiety, hardship, troubles, and suffering and strikes us the way a stone strikes the surface of a lake. The initial impact causes a 'splash' that is followed by a succession of ripples as the stone sinks. Ripples happen as a natural reaction to the pressure whose force of energy must go somewhere, just as it does across the surface of the lake *and* into its depth.

Most people watch the stone and are drawn to the visible effect: the splash and the ripples. They give little attention to the stone below the surface and its effect there. Yet a different effect is happening underneath. Down in the dark, still quietness of our being, the 'stone' sinks until it touches bottom and becomes part of the lake bed.

Awareness is the lake bed. It simply holds everything, sees everything, absorbs everything, and resolves everything *into itself*, all the while remaining silent, motionless, and invisibly aware of being aware.

Identified Awareness

IDENTIFIED awareness is awareness without consciousness of itself. It still contains the substance of awareness but without awareness of itself, which is its most essential aspect.

The mind is a heavy, dense, slow instrument compared to awareness. Consequently, it cannot grasp the rarefied nature of awareness, or see that awareness is always looming so close. It cannot intuit the mysterious quality of being able to be aware of being aware.

It is this last ingredient that goes missing when identification happens.

Mind, Body, and Ego

WHEREAS eastern-oriented teachings refer generally to mind, body and ego, the fourth way tradition describes them in much greater detail. Instead of 'mind' and 'body', the fourth way describes our psychological and physical makeup in terms of four *centers*, two of which comprise the mind and two the body.

The body is viewed as an instinctive center and a moving center. The instinctive center includes all physiological traits such as heartbeat, breathing, circulation, digestion, hormone production, sneezing, yawning—all of the *internal* workings of the body that operate on their own, automatically.

The moving center includes all physical movements such as walking, talking, writing, driving, riding a bike, typing, using tools, playing games—all *external* movements that have to be learned or imitated. The moving center is closely aligned to the instinctive center and they often work together so that, to the unlearned eye, they appear as one—as the 'body'.

In terms of the mind, the fourth way distinguishes between an intellectual and an emotional center which, like their counterparts in the physical body, appear to operate as one but are different.

The intellectual center is the realm of conceptual thought, theories, ideas, information, cataloguing, comparison, analysis, and 'thinking' whereas the emotional center is the engine of 'feelings': personal likes and dislikes, opinions, convictions, prejudices, insistent attitudes, the need to be right, and the desire to be admired and respected.

The distinction of mind and body as four centers provides a nuanced view of the ego where each center generates a different sense of 'I' at different times and in different circumstances: 'I' am hungry, 'I' disagree. 'I' love politics. 'I' hate Martha. Each of these 'I's occupies the ego yet stems from a separate center, and as they displace each other they do so with a camouflage that prevents one 'I' in one center from seeing another 'I' in a different center. Rarely if ever do all the 'I's in all four centers come into contact. Even when they do, they lack the capacity to comprehend their divisive multiplicity.

What this reveals is that the ego is not one thing but rather a complex infrastructure of four centers and thousands of 'I's that are difficult to trace to their source—which is not a single source, but four distinct centers. At the same time, there *is* a single sense of ego behind all four centers; and this is where it gets tricky because that single point is awareness.

The trouble is that awareness is not aware of being aware. Consequently, as soon as an 'I' surfaces, no matter which center it originates from, awareness identifies with it and *becomes* that 'I' until it is replaced by another 'I' in the same or a different center. If there is a contradiction or conflict between different 'I's, awareness *lives* that, too—instead of simply seeing it and being aware of seeing it.

The process of awareness repeatedly and *unconsciously* transforming into each 'I' that manifests accumulates as an overriding sense of 'me' which eastern teachings call the ego. In actuality, there is no ego. The ego is an illusion—a presumption of identity—which derives content from the four centers and fuel from the identification of awareness.

In fourth way terminology, this illusion of ego coalesces as an *internal* image of 'me' which projects itself *externally* in the form of a fabricated or 'false' personality. Everyone then goes around assuming that 'this' is 'me' and presenting 'me' to a world where everyone else is doing the same thing, mutually agreeing to the same illusion, and continuously reinforcing the same in each other.

The spiritual consequences of this culminate when 'I's from different centers come together as negative emotions and then legitimize themselves by expressing negative emotions. When this happens, awareness reaches its most extreme degree of identification where it is completely subsumed by the four centers in the form of a full-blown, self-convincing, self-perpetuating ego.

The reason negative emotions are central to the fourth way approach is because they represent the point where imaginary 'I' (ego) can be brought into focus, contained, and neutralized. This is the point where awareness can then step out of the entire cycle of identification, step into the quiet place of itself, and resurrect itself as pure awareness which is no longer conjoined to mind, body, and ego.

Filtering and Separating Thoughts

KNOWING about the four centers—being able to distinguish between the different parts of mind and body—is useful for separating thought, emotion, sensation, and movement from each other and from awareness.

For example, when a negative emotion is triggered and starts to react, it is possible to break that reaction into separate pieces and thereby weaken the combined effect. When an emotion of anger and blame arises, you can detect not only the burst of energy, but the physical sensation behind it, the mental attitude justifying it, and the emotional feeling of permission you give yourself to express it.

In seeing all this and at the same time realizing awareness as the seer, the threads of a negative emotion start to loosen and unravel. As this happens, the notion of 'me' also loosens to reveal that there is no self behind the veil of negativity.

In truth, there *never* was such a self. It was made up and embroidered.

The Ego and Negative Emotions

NEGATIVE emotions are a psychic phenomenon that doesn't exist in the animal, natural, or mineral worlds because those life forms don't include the mental framework that negative emotions require; the framework where the hologram of the ego takes shape.

In fourth way terminology, it is called 'false personality' or 'imaginary picture of oneself' because it is a psychological phantom that is woven from a mix of sensations, thoughts, and emotions into a reference point of 'me'.

This knot of 'I' and 'me' is where negative emotions form and get reinforced. It is here that they are triggered internally and launched externally as negativity.

Everyone's false personality (ego) builds negative emotions and stores them—fully assembled—for repeated use as psychological weapons of defense and attack, depending on the threat the ego feels it is under. This ego of identity becomes a familiar, easy hook for identification to hold onto.

The Two Ends of Negativity

NEGATIVE emotions are like a stick. On one end is the identification where negative emotions begin. At the other end is their expression where they conclude.

Running the length of the stick is the material comprising a negative emotion: the initial reaction followed by manufacture of the emotion, the rationale behind it, and the justification to express it. At each of these rapid-fire stages, the ego surges.

The transformation of negative emotions can start from either end of the stick. You can not identify (by being aware of being aware) in which case the negative emotion cannot take shape. Or you can start at the other end by not expressing the negative emotion, in which case the ego cannot manifest in the outer world.

You are not trying to suppress negative emotions internally or squash them externally. You are trying to throw light on them internally. From non-expression, you work backwards from withholding the expression of a negative emotion to 'looking within' at the justification, the rationale, and the urge behind it. If you can trace it to its source, you may arrive at the tiny, intense spark that ignited the instant you became identified. At that point you will see the lamp that produced the genie of the ego-hologram.

From one end of the stick, you re-member awareness. From the other end, you dis-member the ego.

Disentangling Negative Emotions

THE mind can disentangle the thinking that supports a negative emotion, but it cannot undo the energy or the sensation behind a negative emotion.

For example, you slip on a wet floor and fall, hurting yourself. Instantaneously the physical sensation of pain ignites an emotion of blame (as a defense mechanism) which elicits the help of the intellect to fashion a 'reason' why you fell—namely that someone else left the floor wet. You then get angry and express negativity.

This is just one example of the habitual reaction that happens whenever things don't go well. And although the mind can rearrange the thinking behind it, only awareness can be above the whole process.

The Feeling of Dread

AT the core of some negative emotions such as anxiety, depression, guilt, and fear there is a sensation of dread. Whether it is slight or intense, it forms at the bottom of our *physical* sense of being and from there seeps into the *emotional* perception of ourselves and the world. This dread is recognizable by its combination of instinctive and emotional ingredients which linger in the body and swirl in the mind with the conviction that this is 'me'.

Whereas impatience, anger, destruction, and violence *ex*plode and poison the outside world, emotions of dread *im*plode and poison our inner world with a disturbing sense of 'I' in the body and mind. And because the dread is solidly anchored in the body, it is difficult for awareness to 'get out'.

Yet awareness is the key because seeing the dread is evidence that you are the seer of it. Anything that can be perceived is not awareness, so no matter how powerful sensations and emotions are, it is possible to wait them out, let them pass, and not grant them identity. How to do that? By accepting it and even cradling it in awareness. By consciously transcending it as it passes *through* awareness. The more you grant identity to strong emotions, be they volatile or slow-burning, the more they will appropriate awareness.

The converse is also true. The more you honor awareness as awareness, the more these sensations and emotions will dissolve into and become awareness.

6

Frequently consider the connection
of all things in the universe.

Marcus Aurelius

The Quiet Place Within

Ripples of Negativity

WHEN something unpleasant happens to us or is said to us, our usual reaction is to recoil from the impact and respond with ripples of negativity. Most people take up temporary residence in their ripples, dwell on them, and hold them up for others to see. Almost no one dives below to absorb the pressure.

The next time a negative emotion flares in you in response to something or someone, instead of putting your identity *into* the negative emotion and expressing it, quietly tuck the negative emotion into awareness. Surround it internally without clinging to it. Cradle it as it sinks into you. Let it carry you to the depth of your being and resolve there *as* awareness, which it will do if you attend to it the right way.

It is in the deep, silent depths of ourselves that negative emotions are transformed into awareness.

Rings and Hooks

NISARGADATTA said, "The world is made of rings. The hooks are all yours. Unbend your hooks." In other words, everything physical and psychological is a ring that can be grabbed by the hook of awareness.

First, the hook grabs the ring (attachment). Then it closes all the way around it (identification). As a result, awareness *becomes* the thing it is aware of, and the thing becomes it; awareness and the object of its perception are fused.

When awareness is aware of being aware, it never forms into a hook. It never forms into anything. It just sees and watches.

The Fire of Negativity

FIRE fighters try to extinguish the fire, minimize the damage, and prevent it from spreading. This is what it means to control the *expression* of negative emotions.

Fire investigators follow up to study the fire's movement and determine the source of ignition. This is what it means to look *inside* and trace negative emotions to their source.

When you trace the roots of negative emotions far enough, you will discover the *same source* behind all of them: a stronghold of 'I' that permeates the mind and body in different forms—different variations of negativity—but always with the same flavor.

When you find this, you have found the core of the ego. But don't do anything to it. Just look at it in its entirety and be aware of seeing it.

The Engine of Negativity

IT feels right to indulge in negative emotions internally, and it feels justifiable to express them externally. Both actions seem as though they will make things different and more according to our preferences.

This is because the force behind all negative emotions is one of the most volatile forms of energy in our mind and body. Within fractions of a second, this energy can form as a combustible mix of physiological reactions, psychological rationale, and physical tension. Together they generate a high-octane thrust that is hard to resist internally and harder to contain externally. Before you know it, you feel negative and are expressing it *in some way*.

Manufacturing and expressing negative emotions may seem like a solution to whatever is bothering you, but apart from making you feel better (by releasing its volatile energy), it does not solve or change anything. All it does is bind awareness more firmly to the mind and body.

Awareness and Negativity

NEGATIVE emotions begin and end with awareness because awareness is there *first* before any negative emotions develop. But instead of being aware of itself, it gets attached to and identifies with negative emotions as they arise in the image of ego.

The ego becomes a filter which *responds to perceptions* internally. This filter is different for each person, but it uses negative emotions the same way in everyone: to reject what it doesn't like and to negate whatever opposes it. It either spits out the perception with an explosive burst, or oozes it out through a slow burn of negative emanations. In both cases it corrupts the 'substance' of awareness which brought the perception in the first place.

By contrast, conscious awareness never reacts or responds. It simply sees things as they are. It can even see itself being corrupted by and discarded *through* negative emotions. But it can't do anything about that until it realizes what it means to be consciously aware.

The Nature of Awareness

AWARENESS is a void of silent, shapeless, motionless consciousness that is aware of being aware. At its source, in its purest form, awareness exists simply as itself.

When it extends itself beyond itself to become aware of other things, it does so in the form of perception, just as the sun extends itself in the form of light.

The sun does not have to extend itself beyond itself. Doing so is an inevitable manifestation of being the sun, yet its light is a different substance than the source which generates the light. That source never leaves itself, even as it jets across the solar system.

The Umbrella of Awareness

IT is easy to take for granted that we reside on the surface of the earth inside a 10,000-ft. tall oxygen tank which comprises a fifth of the earth's atmosphere.

Shrouded in this atmosphere, the ground below our feet appears motionless as it rotates at nearly 26,000 miles an hour, while the earth revolves around the sun at another 66,000 miles per hour. Meanwhile, the solar system is revolving around a distant point in the galaxy which is itself speeding somewhere. Beyond that, science cannot accurately fathom the full extent of distances, speeds, or dimensions of the universe.

Compared to Jupiter and Saturn, the earth is a tiny planet around which nature forms a delicate sheath. Inside this sheath, life plays out one planetary turn at a time over eons, always under the umbrella of awareness.

Abstinence

THE practice of abstinence is interpreted by the mind and body on their terms, according to their idea of sacrifice. In relation to awareness, however, abstinence carries a different meaning.

Due to identification, awareness does not encounter reality directly. Reality is instead filtered by the mind and body. Only when awareness sidesteps (abstains from) the 'person' of mind and body can it exercise its potential as *pure* awareness. This does not mean bypassing the mind and body; it means transcending the feeling of 'I' and 'me' that is perpetuated through identification.

As awareness becomes aware of being aware, it naturally pulls away and abstains from the feeling of 'I'.

Self Denial

ANOTHER practice which is used for religious reasons (as well as by athletes for physical conditioning) is the idea of self-denial: depriving oneself of indulgences for the sake of gaining something else.

As with abstinence, self-denial is conceived by the mind and body as *they* experience it. The esoteric meaning, however, is to not indulge the 'self' behind our person; to deny the sense of 'I' and 'me'. It means awareness refraining from identification so that the mind and body cannot misconstrue themselves as awareness.

The Theatre of the Mind

THE four centers—instinctive and moving in the body, intellectual and emotional in the mind—each occupy their own domain from which they generate a sense of 'I'. Whichever 'I' (or group of 'I's or memories) appears in the moment, it is placed on center stage in the theatre of the mind for awareness to see.

Because awareness is usually unaware of being aware, and because it usually sits in the front row, our thoughts, emotions, and sensations come so close that awareness thinks it *is* the performance and that each performer— each 'I'—is a manifestation of itself.

Only when awareness starts to realize itself as awareness does it step back and see the show as just a show. Only then does it start to disbelieve the performers and lose interest in their repetitive reenactment of the same plots and plights and endings.

Awareness realizes that it has been an unwitting patron of the theatre of our mind, and that it has the option to get up and move to the back of the theater, or to leave altogether and venture into the real world.

Fuel for the Ego

THE body does not like inconvenience or pain, just as the mind does not like confusion or conflict. The ego, on the other hand, likes all of these because they provide the fuel that it thrives on.

What we experience as inconvenience, pain, confusion, and conflict are simply different forms of turbulence in the four centers. And each of us unconsciously uses this turbulence to construct an ego that feels like a sense of self.

When our turbulences are stilled—such as through meditation, yoga, prayer, and even hobbies—the ego does not go away; it just goes dormant until fresh turbulence arises. This is why the ordinary conditions of life offer the best chance to see the workings of the ego.

Every day we encounter some degree of inconvenience, pain, confusion, and conflict, and every day the ego responds by reconfiguring itself *in the same way* (which is why our feeling of self persists day after day).

Awareness resides just behind all this.

Watching the Centers

EACH 'I' that arises in our mind and body (each thought, feeling, sensation, and emotional urge) follows a certain path depending on which centers it comes from.

For example, thoughts stemming from the instinctive center often begin as a sensation in the abdominal area. Even if a pain starts in the head or a limb, it will prompt a sensation in the gut which in turn transcribes that sensation into a thought, such as a thought of concern or worry or fear. Even after instinctive sensations are sent to the brain, they quickly settle in the gut where they percolate and propagate.

Emotional sensations, on the other hand, generally flare in and around the solar plexus and then rise to the head. We feel a sudden 'burst' in the chest followed by a flush of the face and a rapid churning of thoughts in response to whatever prompted the emotion. When the prompt is something strictly emotional—such as a judgment or retaliatory point of view—the sensation continues to circulate in the region of our chest and head.

'I's from the intellectual center are less volatile and more simple in how they form. They originate in the head where they 'spin' and play themselves out. Word puzzles, business analyses, and math problems never find their way below the neck.

Simplest of all the 'I's are those generated by the moving center which arise as urges to move or stop moving, and which manifest through our torso and limbs.

The more conscious awareness is, the more naturally and harmoniously the four centers operate. But even as they operate in tandem, they are never conscious *of themselves.*

Rushing

IT is not necessary to rush through our day and through our life, despite the sense of pressure we feel, which is primarily imposed on us by us. Even when it is imposed by others, it is almost always a derivative of expectations and nothing else.

7

Only in the complete absence of yourself
is there total presence.

Jean Klein

Liberation

AWARENESS is always there; it just loses awareness of being there. But when identification is intense enough, awareness temporarily *disappears* in the thing it is aware of—be it a thought, an emotion, an opinion, a pain, an activity, a person, or a possession.

The result is that awareness gets appropriated by the mind as a sense of 'I', and by the body as a sense of 'me'. The substance of awareness instills identity in the mind and security in the body, and they in turn 'anchor' awareness.

Liberation occurs when awareness, as a result of realizing itself, slips free from these anchors and consciously re-collects and re-members the substance of itself.

The Parts

THE penny, nickel, dime, quarter, and fifty-cent piece are five parts of a dollar but none of them know the dollar. They each operate on their own and sometimes in tandem, but never as a whole dollar. The same is true of the five senses in relation to awareness. This analogy falls short, however, because the five senses never add up to awareness. It would be like five coins adding up to all the money in the world.

The mind thinks, feelings feel, the eyes see, the ears hear, the tongue tastes, the nose smells, and the fingers touch—but all of them function without being aware *of themselves* functioning. Something else is aware of them.

That something else is usually not aware of itself. But when it is aware, that something thinks the mind, feels the feelings, sees the eyes, hears the ears, tastes the tongue, smells the nose, and touches the fingers. None of the senses diminish or go away. They are all enhanced *by* awareness being consciously aware of them.

Higher Centers

WHAT in some traditions is called the enlightenment or self-realization of awareness is called in the fourth way the awakening of higher centers. The term 'higher centers' is meant to distinguish a level of consciousness above and beyond the lower centers (the instinctive, moving, intellectual, and emotional center). Higher centers are also meant to convey two dimensions or depths that awareness reaches.

The 'higher emotional center' in fourth way terminology refers to what Jean Klein called 'affectionate awareness' through which we perceive the wonder and majesty of creation. This is when the simplest things appear to us as sublime, poetic, and wonderful in their form and manifestation. Affectionate awareness marvels at all creation.

The 'higher intellectual center' refers to seeing into reality more deeply and comprehending it more fully. Affectionate appreciation transforms into conscious knowing. It is the same awareness with greater expansion and penetration.

The Whole

AWARENESS perceives that everything is already part of a whole. When we think this way and see things this way, the mind starts to align with awareness and this can prompt awareness to be aware of being aware.

Conscious awareness also perceives that everything is exactly the way it is supposed to be, and that anything is possible—both of which reflect the nature of wholeness.

Only the limited mind would want to think otherwise, and it would only want to do so as an impulse of the ego which is blindly clinging to itself as something separate from the whole. Fortunately, awareness sees even this and recognizes the ego as part of the whole of human existence.

Whole Awareness

ALTHOUGH the concept of awareness is presented to the mind, the mind cannot grasp the truth behind it. That truth is something awareness has to *realize*.

The mind can think about awareness and the body can try to feel awareness, but neither can *be* awareness. Yet neither recognizes its limitation in this respect.

Awareness itself is also a mystery because to be fully conscious it has to retain awareness of itself *and* extend itself as awareness *of* everything else. And it has to do these *at the same time*.

This double awareness is what Mr. Ouspensky inferred with the idea of divided attention, because that is how the mind experiences it— *as attention*. Awareness itself, however, is more than attention, and it is not really two things. It is one whole awareness.

Inner and Outer Worlds

WHEN we gaze at the heavens, we peer into and through the body of the solar system. Conversely, when the sun looks into its solar system, it sees planets the way awareness sees thoughts in our mind.

If the solar system gazes beyond itself, it peers out and into the inner world of the galaxy, and the galaxy does the same in relation to the universe.

This, of course, presumes that the sun and galaxy possess the capacity for self-reflection and conscious self-realization. It is incredible if they do. And whether they do or not, it is incredible that we possess it, and that awareness can come to fruition *through* us.

Awareness and Drugs

AWARENESS is not chemical and is therefore unaffected by chemical substances such as drugs. Although it is true that some drugs can temporarily suspend the mind and neutralize the body so that they are not blocking awareness, drugs never alter awareness itself.

Drugs may also bring more harm than good because when they suspend the mind, they do not necessarily suspend awareness's identification with the mind. Consequently, as the mind becomes unleashed through drugs, awareness identifies with that, which generally has one of two results: either you experience a 'bad trip' or you mistake the experiences of a good trip for awareness, when in reality both experiences are happening to the mind and body, never to awareness itself.

The self-realization of awareness is not a psychedelic experience. It is better. It is simple, lucid, and self-explanatory, and it doesn't end well or badly. It is just stupendously aware.

Caretakers

IF the mind and body can value awareness and relinquish their projected sense of identity—the ego—they can become caretakers of the awareness flowing through them.

This does not mean becoming a dull person or living a dull life. It means facing the reality of life as a human being and yielding this reality to something much higher: to the truth of awareness. Life then takes on immeasurably more value and meaning.

Some people infer this when they 'surrender' their life to god and to god's will. But it usually represents only a shift of the ego and a change of attitude *in the mind*. Existence remains pinned to and focused on the notion of being a person 'here' with god out 'there' watching over 'me'.

Awareness, on the other hand, realizes that it is part of universal awareness, that there is no man in the sky, and that it is already one *with* absolute awareness.

Leaving the Quiet Place

WHY does awareness collapse out of itself and forget to remember itself? Why is it so prone to attachment and so subject to identifying with things *other* than itself? What does this imply about the awareness inherent in human beings?

These questions bring us up against core mysteries of the universe, the purpose of our existence on earth, and the wonder that we can even pose such questions. One explanation behind all of them, however, is that the tiny world of earth and the manifestation of human beings in this world are tied not only to the universe as a whole but to the absolute awareness encompassing it.

Somehow, the awareness of the universe is as breath is to our body. This vast body is constantly 'breathing' awareness in and out. At the same time, in a way that our minds can never comprehend, awareness is *also* the body which is breathing. It is everything and in everything, and everything is it and in it.

From such a perspective, this means that it is not a 'bad' thing for awareness to lapse and slip out of the heart of itself. It is not bad for it to be breathed out and into attachment and, as a result, to identify with—to *become*—the body *of itself.* This is as true on the scale of the entire universe as it is on the scale of one human being. The 'breath' of awareness has to circulate through everything, through all of *itself.*

What is construed as 'bad' is simply the unconscious exhalation and manifestation of awareness, through which it 'loses' itself in and transforms *into* the body of the universe; and, in our case, into the mind and body of a person.

The reverse—the inhalation of awareness—occurs when awareness becomes aware of being aware and through self-realization transforms itself *out of* our body and back into the heart of itself—back into the quiet place within.

But it could not do this or experience this without having left that place. And what makes the human experience so profound is that we provide a crucial turning point for this to happen—or not.

What makes the human experience so extraordinary is that we seem to exist as a turning point in the universe—a spiritual pivot—where awareness can be realized.

Returning to the Quiet Place

PETER Ouspensky said it is very difficult to find the way back to the quiet place within: "If you do it several times you will be able to remember some of the steps, and by the same steps you may come there again. Only you cannot do it after one experience, for you will not remember the way."

He added, "If you find yourself in it again, try to remember how you got there, for sometimes it happens that one finds this place and loses the way there; then again finds it and again loses the way."

Mr. Ouspensky's advice is addressed to the mind yet refers to awareness. It also presents the mind with a puzzle because the mind can look for the quiet place—can look for awareness—but can never find itself *in* the quiet place. The only solution is for the mind to intuit this and start yielding itself to awareness.

Fulfilled

ENVISION the full expanse of the universe with nothing aware of it. Then picture awareness becoming aware, filling the entire universe with conscious awareness.

The same thing happens in the mind and body, and to our entire life, when awareness becomes aware of being aware.

Shall we go on explaining
or shall we be quiet?

Meher Baba